U0111770

大展好書　好書大展
品嘗好書　冠群可期

▲作者的少林拳　Shaolin Boxing of the Author

▲武術雜誌上的耿軍
Geng Jun on the Cover of Wushu Magazine

▲英法武術代表團訪問孟州少林武術院
The Wushu Delegation of France and UK is visiting the Meng zhou Shaolin Wushu Institute

▲作者部分弟子參加武打片拍攝
Parts of students of author take part in fliming Acrobatic fighting film

▲作者與恩師素法大師
The Author and his Teacher Grandmaster Sufa

▲作者指導女兒耿瑞濤練功
The Author is coaching his daughter to practise her skill

▲作者與原國家武術協會主席張耀庭
The Author and the former Chairman of the Chinese Wushu
Association Zhang Yaoting

▲作者的少林拳　Shaolin Boxing of the Author

▲武術雜誌封面上的耿軍
Geng Jun on the Cover of Wushu Magazine

▲作者與恩師素法大師
The Author and his Teacher Grandmaster Sufa

▲ 作者率領國外弟子朝拜少林寺　Author leads foreign students to visit Shaolin Temple

▲作者與武僧教頭德揚師兄在捶譜堂
In Chuipu Hall, the author and his senior fellow apprentice
who is also the wushu monk teacher deyang

▲作者與中國政協副主席萬國權
The Author and the vice Chairman of the Chinese People's Political
Consultative Conference （CPPCC）Wan Guoquan

▲作者傳藝國際黑帶功夫總會
The Author is teaching his Wushu skill in International
Black Belt Kungfu Federation

▲作者指導兒子耿鵬飛練功
The Author is coaching his son Geng Pengfei to practise
his skill

少林傳統功夫漢英對照系列　❻

Shaolin Traditional Kungfu Series Books　❻

# 七星小架

## Seven-star Small Frame

耿　軍　著

**Written by Geng Jun**

大展出版社有限公司

# 作者簡介

　　耿軍（法號釋德君），1968 年 11 月出生於河南省孟州市，係少林寺三十一世皈依弟子。中國武術七段、全國十佳武術教練員、中國少林武術研究會副秘書長、焦作市政協十屆常委、濟南軍區特警部隊特邀武功總教練、洛陽師範學院客座教授、英才教育集團董事長。1989 年創辦孟州少林武術院、2001 年創辦英才雙語學校。先後獲得河南省優秀青年新聞人物、全國優秀武術教育家等榮譽稱號。

　　1983 年拜在少林寺住持素喜法師和著名武僧素法大師門下學藝，成爲大師的關門弟子，後經素法大師引薦，又隨螳螂拳一代宗師李占元、金剛力功于憲華等大師學藝。在中國鄭州國際少林武術節、全國武林精英大賽、全國武術演武大會等比賽中 6 次獲得少林武術冠軍；在中華傳統武術精粹大賽中獲得了象徵少林武術最高榮譽的「達摩杯」一座。他主講示範的 36 集《少林傳統功夫》教學片已由人民體育音像出版社出版發行。他曾多次率團出訪海外，在國際武術界享有較高聲譽。

七星小架

　　他創辦的孟州少林武術院，現已發展成爲豫北地區最大的以學習文化爲主、以武術爲辦學特色的封閉式、寄宿制學校，是中國十大武術教育基地之一。

## Brief Introduction to the Author

Geng Jun（also named Shidejun in Buddhism）, born in Mengzhou City of Henan Province, November 1968, is a ⁻ Bud－dhist disciple of the 31st generation, the 7th section of Chinese Wu shu, national "Shijia" Wu shu coach, Vice Secretary General of China Shaolin Wu shu Research Society, standing committee member of 10th Political Consultative Conference of Jiaozuo City, invited General Kungfu Coach of special police of Jinan Military District, visiting professor of Luoyang Normal University, and Board Chairman of Yingcai Education Group. In 1989, he estab－lished Mengzhou Shaolin Wu shu Institute; in 2001, he estab－lished Yingcai Bilingual School · He has been successively awarded honorable titles of "Excellent Youth News Celebrity of Henan Province" "State Excellent Wu shu Educationalist" etc.

In 1983, he learned Wu shu from Suxi Rabbi, the Abbot of Shaolin Temple, and Grandmaster Sufa, a famous Wu shu monk, and became the last disciple of the

七星小架

Grandmaster. Then recom-mended by Grandmaster Sufa, he learned Wu shu from masters such as Li Zhanyuan, great master of mantis boxing, and Yu Xianhua who specializes in Jingangli gong. He won the Shaolin Wu shu champion for 6 times in China Zhengzhou International Wu shu Festival, National Competition of Wu lin Elites, National Wu shu Performance Conference, etc. and one "Damo Trophy" that symbolizes the highest honor of Shaolin Wu shu in Chinese Traditional Wu shu Succinct Competition. 36 volumes teaching VCD of Shaolin Traditional Wu shu has been published and is -sued by People's Sports Audio Visual Publishing House. He has led delegations to visit overseas for many times, enjoying high reputation in the martial art circle of the world.

Mengzhou Shaolin Wu shu Institute, established by him, has developed into the largest enclosed type boarding school of Yubei（north of Henan Province）area, which takes knowledge as primary and Wu shu as distinctiveness, also one of China's top ten Wu shu education bases.

# 序　言

中華武術源遠流長，門類繁多。

少林武術源自嵩山少林寺，因寺齊名，是我國拳系中著名的流派之一。少林寺自北魏太和十九年建寺以來，已有一千五百多年的歷史。而少林武術也決不是哪一人哪一僧所獨創，它是歷代僧俗歷經漫長的生活歷程，根據生活所需逐步豐富完善而成。

據少林寺志記載許多少林僧人在出家之前就精通武術或慕少林之名而來或迫於生計或看破紅塵等諸多原因削髮爲僧投奔少林，少林寺歷來倡武，並經常派武僧下山，雲遊四方尋師學藝。還請武林高手到寺，如宋朝的福居禪師曾邀集十八家武林名家到寺切磋技藝，推動了少林武術的發展，使少林武術得諸家之長。

本書作者自幼習武，師承素喜、素法和螳螂拳李占元等多位名家，當年如饑似渴在少林寺研習功夫，曾多次在國內外大賽中獲獎。創辦的孟州少林武術院亦是全國著名的武術院校之一，他示範主講的 36 集《少林傳統功夫》教學 VCD 已由人民體育音像出版社發行。

本套叢書的三十多個少林傳統套路和實戰技法是少

林武術的主要內容，部分還是作者獨到心得，很值得一讀，該書還採用漢英文對照，使外國愛好者無語言障礙，爲少林武術走向世界做出了自己的貢獻，亦是可喜可賀之事。

張耀庭題
甲申秋月

# Preface

Chinese Wushu is originated from ancient time and has a long history, it has various styles.

Shaolin Wushu named from the Shaolin Temple of Songshan Mountain, it is one of the famous styles in the Chinese boxing genre. Shaolin temple has more than 1500 years of history since its establishment in the 19th year of North Wei Taihe Dynasty. No one genre of Shaolin Wushu is created solely by any person or monk, but completed gradually by Buddhist monks and common people from generation to generation through long–lasting living course according to the requirements of life. As recording of Record of Shaolin Temple, many Shaolin Buddhist monks had already got a mastery of Wushu before they became a Buddhist monk, they came to Shaolin for tonsure to be a Buddhist monk due to many reasons such as admiring for the name of Shaolin, or by force of life or seeing through thevanity of life. The Shaolin Temple always promotes Wushu and frequently appoints Wushu Buddhist monks to go down the mountain to roam around for searching masters and learning Wushu from them. It also invites

Wushu experts to come to the temple, such as Buddhist monk Fuju of Song Dynasty, it once invited Wushu famous exports of 18 schools to come to the temple to make skill interchange, which promoted the development of Shaolin Wushu and made it absorb advantages of all other schools.

The author learned from many famous exports such as Suxi, Sufa and Li Zhanyuan of Mantis Boxing, he studied Chinese boxing eagerly in Shaolin Temple, and got lots of awards both at home and abroad, he also set up the Mengzhou Shaolin Wushu Institute, which is one of the most famous Wushu institutes around China. He makes demonstration and teaching in the 36 volumes teaching VCD of Shaolin Traditional Wushu, which have been published by Peoples sports Audio Visual publishing house.

There are more than 30 traditional Shaolin routines and practical techniques in this series of books, which are the main content of Shaolin Wushu, and part of which is the original things learned by the author, it is worthy of reading. The series books adopt Chinese and English versions, make foreign fans have no language barrier, and make contribution to Shaolin Wushu going to the world, which is delighting and congratulating thing.

Titled by Zhang Yaoting

# 目　錄
## Contents

七星小架

# 說　明

（一）為了表述清楚，以圖像和文字對動作作了分解說明，練習時應力求連貫銜接。

（二）在文字說明中，除特別說明外，不論先寫或後寫身體的某一部分，各運動部位都要求協調活動、連貫銜接，切勿先後割裂。

（三）動作方向轉變以人體為準，標明前後左右。

（四）圖上的線條是表明這一動作到下一動作經過的線路及部位。左手、左腳及左轉均為虛線（┄┄►）；右手、右腳及右轉均為實線（──►）。

 # Instructions

( i ) In order to explain clearly figures and words are used to describe the actions in multi steps. Try to keep coherent when exercising.

(ii) In the word instruction, unless special instruction, each action part of the body shall act harmoniously and join coherently no matter it is written first or last, please do not separate the actions.

(iii) The action direction shall be turned taking body as standard, which is marked with front, back, left or right.

(iv) The line in the figure shows the route and position from this action to the next action. The left hand, left foot and turn left are all showed in broken line ( ┄┄► ) ; the right hand, right foot and turn right are all showed in real line ( ──► ) .

# 基本步型與基本手型
## Basic stances and Basic hand forms

圖 1

圖 2

圖 3

圖 4

圖 5

圖 6

七星小架

圖 7

圖 8

圖 9

圖 10

圖 11

圖 12

圖 13

圖 14

圖 15

圖 16

圖 17

圖 18

圖 19

圖 20

圖 21

基本步型與基本手型

## 基本步型

　　少林武術中常見的步型有：弓步、馬步、仆步、虛步、歇步、坐盤步、丁步、併步、七星步、跪步、高虛步、翹腳步12種。

　　**弓步**：俗稱弓箭步。兩腿前後站立，兩腳相距本人腳長的4～5倍；前腿屈至大腿接近水平，腳尖微內扣不超過5°；後腿伸膝挺直，腳掌內扣45°。（圖1）

　　**馬步**：俗稱騎馬步。兩腳開立，相距本人腳長的3～3.5倍，兩腳尖朝前；屈膝下蹲大腿接近水平，膝蓋與兩腳尖上下成一條線。（圖2）

　　**仆步**：俗稱單叉，一腿屈膝全蹲，大腿貼緊小腿，膝微外展，另一腿直伸平仆接近地面，腳掌扣緊與小腿成90°夾角。（圖3）

　　**虛步**：又稱寒雞步。兩腳前後站立，前後相距本人腳長的2倍；重心移至後腿，後腿屈膝下蹲至大腿接近水平，腳掌外擺45°；前腿腳尖點地，兩膝相距10公分。（圖4）

　　**歇步**：兩腿左右交叉，靠近全蹲；前腳全腳掌著地，腳尖外展，後腳腳前掌著地，臀部微坐於後腿小腿上。（圖5）

　　**坐盤步**：在歇步的形狀下，坐於地上，後腿的大小腿外側和腳背均著地。（圖6）

丁步：兩腿併立，屈膝下蹲，大腿接近水平，一腳尖點地靠近另一腳內側腳窩處。（圖7）

併步：兩腿併立，屈膝下蹲，大腿接近水平。（圖8）

七星步：七星步是少林七星拳和大洪拳中獨有的步型。一腳內側腳窩內扣於另一腳腳尖，兩腿屈膝下蹲，接近水平。（圖9）

跪步：又稱小蹬山步。兩腳前後站立，相距本人腳長的2.5倍，前腿屈膝下蹲，後腿下跪，接近地面，後腳腳跟離地。（圖10）

高虛步：又稱高點步。兩腳前後站立，重心後移，後腿腳尖外擺45°，前腿腳尖點地，兩腳尖相距一腳距離。（圖11）

翹腳步：在七星螳螂拳中又稱七星步，兩腿前後站立，相距本人腳長的1.5倍，後腳尖外擺45°，屈膝下蹲，前腿直伸，腳跟著地，腳尖微內扣。（圖12）

## 基本手型

少林武術中常見的手型有拳、掌、鉤3種。

拳：

分為平拳和透心拳。

平拳：平拳是武術中較普遍的一種拳型，又稱方拳。四指屈向手心握緊，拇指橫屈扣緊食指。（圖

13）

　　**透心拳**：此拳主要用於打擊心窩處，故名。四指併攏捲握，中指突出拳面，拇指扣緊抵壓中指梢節處。（圖 14）

　　**掌**：

　　分為柳葉掌、八字掌、虎爪掌、鷹爪掌、鉗指掌。

　　**柳葉掌**：四指併立，拇指內扣。（圖 15）

　　**八字掌**：四指併立，拇指張開。（圖 16）

　　**虎爪掌**：五指分開，彎曲如鉤，形同虎爪。（圖 17）

　　**鷹爪掌**：又稱鎖喉手，拇指內扣，小指和無名指彎曲扣於掌心處，食指和中指分開內扣。（圖 18）

　　**鉗指掌**：五指分開，掌心內含。（圖 19）

　　**鉤**：

　　分為鉤手和螳螂鉤。

　　**鉤手**：屈腕，五指自然內合，指尖相攏。此鉤使用較廣，武術中提到的鉤均為此鉤。（圖 20）

　　**螳螂鉤**：又稱螳螂爪，屈腕成腕部上凸，無名指、小指屈指內握，食指、中指內扣，拇指梢端按貼於食指中節。（圖 21）

# Basic stances

基本步型與基本手型

Usual stances in Shaolin Wushu are: bow stance, horse stance, crouch stance, empty stance, rest stance, cross–legged sitting, T –stance, feet –together stance, seven –star stance, kneel stance, high empty stance, and toes–raising stance, these twelve kinds.

Bow stance: commonly named bow –and –arrow stance. Two feet stand in tandem, the distance between two feet is about four or five times of length of one´s foot; the front leg bends to the extent of the thigh nearly horizontal with toes slightly turned inward by less than 5°; the back leg stretches straight with the sole turned inward by 45°. ( Figure 1 )

Horse stance: commonly named riding step. two feet stand apart, the distance between two feet is 3~3.5 times of length of one´s foot, with tiptoes turned forward; bend knees to squat downward, with thighs nearly horizontal, knees and two tiptoes in line. ( Figure 2 )

Crouch stance: commonly named single split. Bend the knee of one leg and squat entirely with thigh very close to lower leg and knee outspread slightly; straighten the other leg and crouch horizontally close to floor, keep the sole turned inward and forming an included angle of 90° with lower leg. ( Figure 3 )

Empty stance: also named cold –chicken stance. Two feet stand in tandem, the distance between two feet is 2 times of length of one´s foot; transfer the barycenter to back leg, bend the knee of the back leg and squat downward to the extent of the thigh nearly horizontal, with the sole turned outward by 45°; keep the tiptoe of front leg on the ground, with distance between two knees of 10cm. ( Figure 4 )

Rest stance: cross the two legs at left and right, keep them close and entirely squat; keep the whole sole of the front foot on the ground with tiptoes turned outward, the front sole of the back foot on the ground, and buttocks slightly seated on the lower leg of the back leg. ( Figure 5 )

Cross–legged sitting: in the posture of rest stance, sit on the ground, with the outer sides of the thigh and lower leg of the back leg and instep on the ground. ( Figure 6 )

T–stance: two legs stand with feet together, bend knees and squat to the extent of the thighs nearly horizontal, with one tiptoe on the ground and close to inner side of the fossa of the other foot. ( Figure 7 )

Feet–together stance: two legs stand with feet together, bend knees and squat to the extent of the thigh nearly horizontal. ( Figure 8 )

Seven–star stance: Seven–star step is a unique step form in Shaolin Seven–star Boxing and Major Flood Boxing. Keep the inner side of the fossa of one foot turned inward onto tiptoe of the other foot, bend two knees and squat nearly horizontal. ( Figure 9 )

Kneel stance: also named small mountaineering stance. Two feet stand in tandem, the distance between two feet is 2.5

times of length of one´s foot, bend knee of the front leg and squat, kneel the back leg close to the floor, with the heel of back foot off the floor. ( Figure 10 )

High empty stance: also named high point stance. Two feet stand in tandem. Transfer the barycenter backward, turn the tiptoe of the back leg outward by $45°$, with tiptoe of front leg on the ground, and the distance between two tiptoes is length of one foot. ( Figure 11 )

Toes –raising stance: also named seven –star stance in Seven –star Mantis Boxing. Two legs stand in tandem, and the distance between two legs is 1.5 times of length of one´s foot. Keep the tiptoe of back leg turned outward by $45°$, bend knees and squat, straighten the front leg with heel on the ground and tiptoe turned inward slightly. ( Figure 12 )

## Basic hand forms

Usual hand forms in Shaolin Wushu are: fist, palm and hook, these three kinds.

Fist: classified into straight fist and heart–penetrating fist.

Flat fist: a rather common fist form in Wushu, also named square fist. Hold the four fingers tightly toward the palm, and horizontally bend the thumb to button up the fore finger. ( Figure 13 )

Heart –penetrating fist: mainly used for striking the heart part. Put four fingers together and coil –hold them, the middle finger thrusts out the striking surface of the fist, the thumb

buttons up and presses the end and joint of the middle finger. ( Figure 14 )

Palm: classified into willow leaf palm, splay palm, tiger's claw palm, eagle's claw palm, fingers clamping palm.

Willow leaf palm: palm with four fingers up and thumb turned inward. ( Figure 15 )

Eight – shape palm: palm with four fingers up and thumb splay. ( Figure 16 )

Tiger's claw palm: palm with five fingers apart, bent as hook and like tiger's claw. ( Figure 17 )

Eagle's claw palm: also named throat locking hand, with the thumb turned inward, the little finger and middle finger turned onto palm, fore finger and middle finger apart and turned inward. ( Figure 18 )

Fingers clamp palm: palm with five fingers apart and palm drawn in. ( Figure 19 )

Hook: classified into hook hand and mantis hook.

Hook hand: bend the wrist, five fingers drawn in naturally with fingertips together. This hook is used in wide range, the hook mentioned in Wushu refers to this. ( Figure 20 )

Mantis hook: also named mantis' claw, bend wrist into wrist bulge upward, the ring finger and little finger bend to hold inward, with fore finger and fore middle finger turned inward and end of thumb pressed on the middle joint of the fore finger. ( Figure 21 )

# 七星小架套路簡介

## Brief Introduction to the Routine Seven-star Small Frame

七星小架是少林寺較古老的拳術之一，更是少林小架拳法的代表套路。其套路短小精悍，結構嚴謹，功架小巧，靈活多變，發力脆快，氣勢逼人，制敵於方寸之間，充分體現了「守如貓，動如虎」「拳打臥牛之地」的少林拳法風格，是不可多得的優秀套路。

Seven-Star small frame is one of the ancient boxing skills, especially the representative routine of shaolin small frame boxing. This routine is brief, flexible and changeful, with strict structure, smart frame, crisp and quick force exert and pressing vigor, thus it can overwhelm the enemies quickly. This routine, as a difficultly accessed excellent routine, embodies the style of shaoling boxing, ie. "defend as cat, act as tiger" and "fist striking the place where the cattle lies".

# 七星小架套路動作名稱
## Action Names of Routine Seven-star Small Frame

### 第一段　Section One

1. 預備勢　Prepatatory posture
2. 縮身七星　Shrink body in seven-star stance
3. 提膝挑手　Lift knee and raise hand
4. 護膝沖拳　Guard knee and thrust fist
5. 馬步截拳　Intercept with fist in horse stance
6. 裏裹手　Wrap the hand inward
7. 馬步截拳　Intercept with fist in horse stance
8. 馬步撞肘　Strike with elbow in horse stance
9. 弓步扳手　Press hand in bow stance
10. 十字彈腿　Cross snap kick
11. 縮身七星　Shrink body in seven-star stance
12. 上步踩腳雞形步　Step forward and slap foot into chicken-shape stance

### 第二段　Section Two

13. 左右雞形步　Left and right chicken-shape stance

七星小架套路動作名稱

14. 回身頂肘　Turn body and thrust elbow

15. 縮身七星　Shrink body in seven-star stance

16. 十字彈腿　Cross snap kick

17. 縮身七星　Shrink body in seven-star stance

18. 滾身三沖拳　Roll body and punch three times

19. 回身頂肘　Turn body and thrust elbow

20. 縮身七星　Shrink body in seven-star stance

## 第三段　Section Three

21. 十字彈腿　Cross snap kick

22. 縮身七星　Shrink body in seven-star stance

23. 護耳掌　Ear-guarding palm

24. 震腳盤肘　Stamp foot and bend elbow

25. 外擺腿　Swing leg outward

26. 弓步沖拳　Thrust fist in bow stance

27. 馬步截拳　Intercept with fist in horse stance

28. 裏裹手　Wrap the hand inward

## 第四段　Section Four

29. 馬步截拳　Intercept with fist in horse stance

30. 馬步撞肘　Strike with elbow in horse stance

31. 弓步扳手　Press hand in bow stance

32. 十字彈腿　Cross snap kick

33. 縮身七星　Shrink body in seven-star stance

七星小架

34. 二起腳　Jumping kick twice

35. 十字沖拳　Thrust cross fists

36. 縮身七星　Shrink body in seven–star stance

37. 上步兩沖拳　Step forward and punch twice

38. 馬步剪子手　Scissors hand in horse stance

39. 馬步七星　Seven–star in horse stance

40. 收勢　Closing form

# 七星小架套路動作圖解

## Action Illustrtion of Routine Seven-star Small Frame

七星小架套路動作圖解

圖 1

## 第一段　Section One

### 1. 預備勢　Preparatory Posture

(1)兩腳併立；兩手自然下垂，成立正姿勢；目視前方。（圖1）

(1)Bring two feet together, the two hands drop nat–urally, stand at attention. Eyes look forward.〔Figure 1〕

圖 2

(2)上動不停。左腳向左開一步，與肩同寬；雙手自身體兩側屈肘抱拳於腰間，拳心向上；目視左方。（圖 2）

　　要點：挺胸塌腰，頭正頸直；抱拳迅速，挺胸收腹。

七星小架套路動作圖解

(2)Keep the above action, the left foot takes a step leftward, the two feet shall be shoulder –width apart. Bend the elbows from both sides of the body and hold the fists on the waist with the fist–palm up. Eyes look leftward. ( Figure 2 )

Key points: keep the chest out and waist lowered,  with head being correctitude and neck straight. Lift the chest, draw in the abdomen and hold fists quickly.

圖 3

## 2. 縮身七星
Shrink body in seven-star stance

接上勢。身體左轉 90°，上右腳，腳內側裏扣，左腳尖裏側成七星步；雙拳變掌；身體下蹲；同時，左掌經右臂外側立掌於右肩上方；右掌直臂向裏格掌於

要點：上步、下蹲和立掌要協調連貫。

Follow the above posture, turn the body 90° to the left. The right foot steps forward, the inner side of the foot turns inward. The left tiptoe turns inward into seven–star stance, change the two fists into palms. The body squats, at the same time, place the left standing palm above the right shoulder; parry the right palm inward to the front of the right knee, keep the palm inward and the fingers down. Eyes look forward. ( Figure 3 )

Key points: stepping forward, squatting and standing palm shall be harmony and coherent.

七星小架

圖4

### 3. 提膝挑手
### Lift knee and raise hand

接上勢。起身，提右膝，腳尖向下，左腿挺膝直立；同時，右掌屈肘，從懷裏向上挑掌，掌心向左，高與腭平；左掌附於右肘內側；目視右掌。（圖4）

要點：提膝與挑掌要同時進行，乾脆俐落，快速有力。

七星小架套路動作圖解

Follow the above posture, stand up and raise the right knee with toes downward; the left leg stands upright. At the same time, bend the right elbow and raise the palm upward with the palm leftward, at chin level; keep the left palm close to the inner side of the right elbow. Eyes look at the right palm. ( Figure 4 )

Key points: lifting knee and raising palm shall be done simultaneously, coming straight to the point without the slightest hesitation, quickly and forcefully.

七星小架

圖 5

## 4. 護膝沖拳　Guard knee and thrust fist

(1)接上勢。左掌變拳回抱腰間；右掌從懷裏向下裹膝；目視右下方。（圖5）

(1)Follow the above posture, change the left palm into fist, draw back the fist and hold it on the waist; the right palm wraps the knee downward from the bosom. Eyes look right downward. 〔Figure 5〕

七星小架套路動作圖解

圖 6

(2)上動不停。右轉身 90°；右手向右摟抓成拳，回抱腰間；同時，右腳向前落步成右弓步；左拳從腰際向前沖出，拳心沖下，高與肩平；目視前方。（圖 6）

要點：沖拳要擰腰抖肩發力，力達拳面。

(2) Keep the above action, turn the body 90° to the right. Grab the right hand rightward into fist, draw the fist back and hold it on the waist, at the same time, the right foot lands forward into right bow stance; punch the left fist forward from the waist, keep the fist–palm down and the fist–hole rightward, at shoulder height. Eyes look forward.（Figure 6）

Key points: when punching the fist, twist the waist and send the shoulders to apply force that shall reach the striking surface of the fist.

七星小架

圖 7

## 5. 馬步截拳　Intercept with fist in horse stance

（1）接上勢。左轉身 90°成馬步；左拳變掌，經面前向左肩格擋；目視左掌前方。（圖 7）

(1) Follow the above posture, turn the body 90° to the left into horse stance. Change the left fist into palm and parry it to the left shoulder through the front of faces. Eyes look at the front of the left fist forward.（Figure 7）

圖 8

(2)上動不停。左掌變拳回抱腰間；右拳屈肘向右下方截拳，拳心向下，拳眼向左；目視右拳。（圖8）

要點：動作輕靈迅捷，截拳要抖肩發力。

(2) Keep the above action, change the left palm into fist, draw the fist back and hold it on the waist, bend the right elbow to punch the fist right downward, keep the fist-palm down and the fist-hole leftward. Eyes look at the right fist.〔Figure 8〕

Key points: the action shall be light and quick, when punching the fist down, send the shoulder to apply force.

圖 9

## 6. 裹裏手
## Wrap the hand inward

(1)接上勢。起身，左轉身 90°，同時提右腳；右拳直臂內旋；目視前下方。（圖 9）

七星小架套路動作圖解

(1) Follow the above posture, stand up, turn the body to 90° to the left. At the same time, raise the right foot. Rotate right hand inward with arm straight. Eyes look down ahead. (Figure 9)

圖 10

　(2)上動不停。身體下蹲，右腳併步震腳；同時，右手裹於雙膝前；左拳回抱於腰間，拳心向右；目視右手。（圖 10、圖 10 附圖）

　要點：震腳要有力，裹手寸勁。

圖 10 附圖

(2) Keep the above action, squat the body. Put the right foot together with the left one and stamp. At the same time, the right hand wraps in front of the two knees; draw back the left fist and hold it on the waist. Keep the fist-palm rightward. Eyes look at the right hand. ( Figure 10, Attached figure 10 )

Key points: stamping shall be forceful, wrap the hand with very short strength.

圖 11

## 7. 馬步截拳　Intercept with fist in horse stance

接上勢。右腳向右開步成馬步；同時，右拳經胸前向右下方截拳，拳心向下，拳眼向左，力達前臂外沿；目視右拳。（圖 11）

要點：截拳要抖肩發力，短促有力。

Follow the above posture, the right foot steps rightward into horse stance. At the same time, chop right downward with the right fist through the front of the chest, keep the fist–palm down and the fist –hole leftward, the strength shall reach the outer edge of the forearm. Eyes look at the right fist.（Figure 11）

Key points: when intercepting down with the fist, send shoulder to apply force, transiently and forcefully.

圖12

## 8. 馬步撞肘　Strike with elbow in horse stance

接上勢。右拳屈肘回收於胸前，向右撞肘，肘尖
向右，拳心向下，臂與肩平；左拳仍抱於腰間；馬步
不變；目視右方。（圖12）

要點：撞肘要快速短促，擰腰抖肩發力。

Follow the above posture, bend the right fist and draw it
back to the front of the chest, strike the elbow rightward, keep
the elbow joint rightward and the fist–palm downward, the arm
shall be at shoulder height. Keep the left fist held on the waist in
horse stance. Eyes look rightward.（Figure 12）

Key points: striking with the elbow shall be quick and
transient, twist the waist and send shoulder to apply force.

圖 13

## 9. 弓步扳手
## Press hand in bow stance

接上勢。右轉身 90°成右弓步，重心前移；右拳變掌，旋臂轉腕，由胸前向前反背扳掌，掌心斜向內，掌指斜向上，掌指與眼同平；左拳仍抱於腰間；目視右掌。（圖 13）

要點：反背扳掌要短促而快速，抖肩發力。

七星小架套路動作圖解

Follow the above posture, turn the body 90° to the right, move the barycenter forward. Change the right fist into palm, rotate the arm and turn over the wrist to turn round the palm forward through the front of the chest, keep the palm inward aslant and the fingers upward aslant, the fingers shall be at eye height. Keep the left fist held on the waist. Eyes look at the right palm. ( Figure 13 )

Key points: turning round the palm shall be transient and quick, send shoulder to apply force.

圖 14

## 10. 十字彈腿　Cross snap kick

（1）接上勢。右掌屈臂外旋上挑，掌與肩平；左拳變掌，附於與右臂內側肘窩處；弓步不變；目視前方。（圖 14）

(1) Follow the above posture, bend the left arm out-ward and raise the right palm, the palm shall be at shoulder height, change the left fist into palm and keep it close to the fossa at the inner side of the right arm in bow stance. Eyes look forward. (Figure 14)

七星小架套路動作圖解

圖 15

(2)上動不停。右掌向外、向下攪手於腹前；弓步不變；目視右手。（圖 15）

(2) Keep the above action, stir the right hand outward to downward in front of the chest. Keep in bow stance. Eyes look at the right hand.〔Figure 15〕

七星小架

圖 16

　　(3)上動不停。微起身；右掌向上屈臂收於左腋下；左掌下按於腹前；弓步不變；目視前下方。（圖16）

　　(3) Keep the above action, raise the body slightly, bend the right arm upward and draw it back under the left armpit, press the left palm in front of the abdomen and keep in bow stance. Eyes look downward ahead. 〔Figure 16〕

圖 17

（4）上動不停。身體下蹲；右掌向前反背擊出；左掌直臂向後勾摟，掌心向上；左腳屈膝提起，向前呈水平彈踢，腳面繃直，右腿屈膝站立；目視前方。（圖 17）

要點：彈提要繃直腳面，抖肩發力，力達腳尖。

(4) Keep the above action, squat the body. Swing the right palm forward with backhand; grab left palm backward while the left arm is straight, keep the fist–centre up. Bend the left knee to raise the left foot, horizontally kick it forward, stretch the instep straight. The right leg stands with the knee bent. Eyes look forward. ( Figure 17 )

Key points: when kicking, stretch the instep straight, send the shoulders to apply force that shall reach the tiptoe.

圖 18

## 11. 縮身七星
### Shrink body in seven-star stance

接上勢。左腳落地，右腳內側裏扣，左腳尖裏側成七星步；同時，身略右轉，身體下蹲，重心前移；左掌直臂向裏格掌於左膝前；右手屈肘附於左肩上；目視左前方。（圖18）

要點：動作要協調連貫，輕靈快速。

七星小架套路動作圖解

Follow the above posture, the left foot falls to the ground; turn the inner side of the right foot inward. Turn the left tiptoe inward into seven–star stance. At the same time, slightly turn the body to the right, squat the body and shift the barycenter forward. Parry inward with the left palm in front of the left knee while the left arm is straight; bend the right elbow and keep it close to the left shoulder. Eyes look left forward. ( Figure 18 )

Key points: the action shall be harmony and coherent, light and quick.

圖 19

### 12. 上步踩腳雞形步　Step forward and slap foot into chicken-shape stance

(1)接上勢。起身，左腳上步；雙手抱拳於腰間，拳心向上；目視前方。（圖 19）

(1)Follow the above posture, raise the body, the left foot steps forward; hold the two fists on the waist with the fist-palms up. Eyes look forward.（Figure 19）

圖 20

(2)上動不停。左腿直立支撐，右腿屈膝提起，向前、向上彈踢，腳尖與肩同高；右拳變掌，向前拍擊腳面，手與肩平；目視右腳。（圖 20）

(2) Keep the above action, the left leg stands straight alone; bend the right knee to kick the right foot upward ahead, the tiptoe shall be at shoulder height. Change the right fist into palm and slap the instep forward, the hand shall be at shoulder height. Eyes look at the right foot.〔Figure 20〕

七星小架

圖 21

(3)上動不停。右腳落地，同時右轉身 180°；右掌
落於右側；左掌屈肘向前上托掌，掌心向上；目視前
方。（圖 21）

要點：彈踢和轉身要連貫協調，快速有力。

(3) Keep the above action, the right foot falls to the ground,
at the same time, turn the body 180° to the right. The right palm
drops at the right side of the body; bend the left elbow to lift the
palm forward with the palm up. Eyes look forward.（Figure
21）

Key points: snap kick and body turn shall be coherent and
harmony, quick and forceful.

圖 22

# 第二段 Section Two

## 13. 左右雞形步
### Left and right chicken-shape stance

(1)接上勢。左手向身後摟掛；右手屈肘，向前、向上托掌，掌心向上；同時，左腳向前、向右搓地提膝，右腿彎曲支撐；目視前方。（圖 22）

(1)Follow the above posture, grab and hang the left hand behind the body; bend the right elbow to lift the palm forward with the palm up. At the same time, the left foot shuffles rightward ahead and lifts the knee; the right bent leg stands alone. Eyes look forward.（Figure 22）

圖23

(2)上動不停。左腳向左前方落地；右手向身後摟掛；左手屈肘，向前、向上托掌；同時，右腳向前、向左搓地提膝，左腿彎曲支撐；目視前方。（圖23）

(2) Keep the above action, the left lands to the ground leftward ahead. Grab and hang the right hand behind the body; bend the left elbow to lift the palm forward. At the same time, the right foot shuffles ground rightward ahead to lift the knee; the left bent leg stands alone. Eyes look forward.（Figure 23）

圖 24

　(3)上動不停。右腳向右前方落地；左手向身後摟掛；右手屈肘，向前、向上托掌；同時，左腳向前、向右搓地提膝，右腿彎曲支撐；目視前方。（圖 24）

　要點：雞形步與摟掛、托掌要同時進行，動作連貫，協調一致。

(3) Keep the above action, the right foot lands to the ground rightward ahead. Grab and hang the left hand behind the body; bend the right elbow to left the palm forward. At the same time, the left foot shuffles rightward ahead to lift the knee; the bent right leg stands alone. Eyes look forward. ﹝ Figure 24 ﹞

　Key points: change into chicken–shape step, grabbing and hanging, lifting the palm shall be completed sim –ultaneously, the action shall be coherent, harmony and consistent.

七星小架

圖 25

## 14. 回身頂肘
### Turn body and thrust elbow

(1)接上勢。左腳向前落步，右轉身 90°，右腳回收，腳內側裏扣，左腳尖裏側，雙腿微屈；右掌變拳，左掌附於右拳面；目視右拳。（圖 25）

七星小架套路動作圖解

(1) Follow the above posture, the left foot falls for-ward. Turn the body 90° to the right, draw back the right foot. Turn the inner side of the foot inward, keep the left tiptoe inward, and slightly bend two legs. Change the right palm into fist, keep the left palm close to the right fist-plane. Eyes look at the right fist. ( Figure 25 )

圖 26

　　(2)上動不停。左掌附於右拳面，同時，抬左臂向右上方頂肘；下肢動作不變；目視右前上方。（圖26、圖26附圖）

　　要點：頂肘要抖肩發力，短促有力，力達肘尖。

圖 26 附圖

(2) Keep the above action, keep the left palm close to the right fist-plane. At the same time, lift the left arm to thrust the elbow right upward. Keep the action of the lower limb. Eyes look right upward ahead. ( Figure 26, Attached figure 26 )

Key points: when thrusting the elbow, send the shoulders to apply force ransiently and forcefully, the force reach the elbow joint.

圖 27

## 15. 縮身七星　Shrink body in seven–star stance

接上勢。身體下蹲成七星步，同時右轉身；左手屈肘立掌於右肩前；右掌直臂向前下方插掌，掌心向內，掌指向下；目視前方。（圖 27）

Follow the above posture, squat the body into seven–star step. At the same time, turn the body to the right, bend the left elbow to stand the palm in front of the right shoulder; insert the right palm downward ahead with the right arm straight, keep the palm inward and the fingers down. Eyes look forward.（Figure 27）

圖 28

## 16. 十字彈腿　Cross snap kick

(1)接上勢。右掌向上挑掌；下肢動作不變；目平視前方。（圖 28）

(1)Follow the above posture, thrust the right palm upward, keep the action of the lower limb.　Eyes horizontally look forward.（Figure 28）

七星小架

圖 29

(2)上動不停。右掌向外、向下旋轉；目視右手。
（圖 29）

(2)Keep the above action, rotate the right palm outward and
downward.  Eyes look at the right hand.〔Figure 29〕

七星小架套路動作圖解

圖 30

(3)上動不停。右掌屈臂收於左腋下；左掌下按於腹前；目視前下方。（圖 30）

(3) Keep the above action, bend the right arm and draw back the right palm under the left armpit, press the left palm downward to the front of the abdomen. Eyes look downward ahead. ( Figure 30 )

七
星
小
架

圖 31

(4)上動不停。右腿屈膝支撐，左腳向前、向上呈
水平彈踢；同時，右掌反背向前擊出；左手直臂向後
勾摟；目視前方。（圖 31）

(4) Keep the above action, the right leg bends and stands
alone; the left foot horizontally kicks upward ahead. At the same
time, strike forward the right backhand palm, grab the left hand
backward with the left arm straight. Eyes look forward.（Figure
31）

圖 32

## 17. 縮身七星　Shrink body in seven-star stance

接上勢。左腳落地，右腳內側裏扣，左腳尖裏側成七星步，同時身體下蹲，略右轉；右掌屈肘立掌於左肩上方；左掌直臂向裏格掌於左膝前；目視左方。（圖 32）

Follow the above posture, the left foot falls to the ground, turn the inner side of the right foot inward with the left tiptoe inward into seven-star stance. At the same time, squat the body and slightly turn to the right. Bend the right elbow and stand the right palm above the left shoulder; parry inward with the left palm to the front of the left knee with the left arm straight. Eyes look leftward.（Figure 32）

圖 33

## 18. 滾身三沖拳
## Roll body and punch three times

(1)接上勢。左腳向左跨一步成馬步；同時，左手抱拳於胸前；右掌下按於左拳前，掌心向下；目視左拳。（圖 33）

(1) Follow the above posture, the left foot strides a step leftward into horse stance. At the same time, hold the left fist in front of the chest; press the right palm downward before the left fist with the palm down. Eyes look at the left fist.〔Figure 33〕

七星小架套路動作圖解

圖 34

(2)上動不停。右拳回抱腰間；同時，左擰身成左弓步；左拳向前內旋沖出，拳心向下，拳眼向右，高與肩平；目視前方。（圖 34）

(2) Keep the above action, draw back the right fist and hold it on the waist, at the same time, twist the body to the left into left bow stance; rotate the left fist inward and punch it forward, keep the fist-palm downward and the fist-hole rightward, at shoulder height. Eyes look forward.（Figure 34）

圖 35

(3)上動不停。上右腳，同時；左轉身 180°成馬步；右手抱拳於胸前；左掌在身體右側下按於右拳前，掌心向下；目視右拳。（圖 35）

(3) Keep the above action, the right foot steps forward. At the same time, turn the body 180° to the left into horse stance. Hold the right fist in front of the chest; press the left palm at the right side of the body to the front of the right fist with palm down. Eyes look at the right fist.（Figure 35）

圖 36

（4）上動不停。右擰身成右弓步；左掌變拳回抱腰間同時，右拳向前內旋沖出，拳面向前，拳眼向左，高與肩平；目視前方。（圖 36）

(4) Keep the above action, twist the body to the right into right bow stance. Change left palm into fist, draw it back and hold it on the waist. At the same time, rotate the right fist inward and punch it forward, keep the fist－plane forward and the fist－hole leftward, at shoulder height. Eyes look forward.（Figure 36）

圖 37

(5)上動不停。左腳向前上步，身體下蹲成馬步；
左手抱拳於胸前；右掌按於左拳前，掌心向下；目視
左拳。（圖 37）

(5) Keep the above action, the left foot steps for-ward,
squat the body into horse stance. Hold the left fist in front of the
chest; press the right palm at the left side of the body to the front
of the left fist with the palm down. Eyes look at the left fist.
（Figure 37）

七星小架套路動作圖解

圖 38

(6)上動不停。左擰身成左弓步；右手變拳回抱腰間同時，左拳向前內旋沖出，拳面向前，拳眼向右，高與肩平；目視前方，發「嗯」聲。（圖 38）

(6) Keep the above action, twist the body to the left into left bow stance. Change right hand into fist, draw it back and hold it on the waist. At the same time, rotate the left fist inward and punch it forward, keep the fist–plane forward and the fist–hole rightward, at shoulder height. Eyes look forward, make the sound of ″en″. ( Figure 38 )

圖 39

## 19. 回身頂肘　Turn body and thrust elbow

(1)接上勢。抬左腳向前落步，右轉身，右腳回收，右腳內側裏扣，左腳尖裏側，雙腿微屈；右掌變拳；左掌附於右拳面；目視左後方。（圖 39）

(1) Follow the above posture, raise the left foot and fall forward, turn the body to the right, draw back the right foot. Turn the inner side of the right foot inward, turn the left tiptoe inward, and bend the two legs slightly. Change the right palm into fist, keep the left palm close to the right fist–plane. Eyes  look left backward.（Figure 39）

七星小架套路動作圖解

圖 40

(2)上動不停。右臂屈肘向右上方頂肘，肘尖斜向上；左掌仍附於右拳面；下肢姿勢不變；目視右上方。（圖 40）

要點：頂肘要抖肩發力，迅猛連貫。

(2) Keep the above action, bend the right elbow to thrust it right upward with the elbow joint upward aslant, keep the left palm close to the right fist–plane. Keep the posture of the lower limb. Eyes look right upward. 〔Figure 40〕

Key points: when thrusting the elbow, send the shoulders to apply force swiftly and coherently.

圖 41

## 20. 縮身七星　Shrink body in seven-star stance

接上勢。身體下蹲成七星步；左手經胸前屈肘立掌於右肩前，掌心向右；右掌直臂向前、向下插掌，掌心向內，掌指向下；目視右前方。（圖 41）

要點：上步、下蹲和立掌要協調連貫。

七星小架套路動作圖解

Follow the above posture, squat the body into seven-star stance. Bend the left elbow to stand the left palm in front of the right shoulder with the palm rightward; insert the right palm downward ahead with the right arm straight, keep the palm inward and the fingers down. Eyes look right forward. ( Figure 41 )

Key points: stepping forward, squatting the body and standing palm shall be harmony and coherent.

圖 42

# 第三段　Section Three

### 21. 十字彈腿　Cross snap kick

⑴接上勢。右掌外旋向上挑起，掌心向左；左掌屈肘附於右肘；下肢姿勢不變；目視右掌。（圖 42）

⑴Follow the above posture, rotate the right palm outward and raise it upward with the palm leftward; bend the left elbow and keep the left palm close to the right elbow. Keep the posture of the lower limb. Eyes look at the right palm.（Figure 42）

圖 43

(2)上動不停。右掌外旋向下至腹前；下肢姿勢不
變；目視前下方。（圖 43）

(2) Keep the above action, rotate the righe palm outward
down to the front of the abdomen, and keep the posture of the
lower limbs. Eyes look downward ahead.〔Figure 43〕

七星小架

圖 44

（3）上動不停。右掌收於左腋下；左掌向下按於腹前；下肢姿勢仍不變；目視左掌。（圖 44）

(3) Keep the above action, draw back the right palm under the left armpit; press the left palm to the front of the abdomen. Keep the posture of the lower limb. Eyes look at the left palm.
(Figure 44 )

七星小架套路動作圖解

圖 45

(4)上動不停。右掌從左腋下經胸前向前反背擊出；同時，身體略下蹲，右腳屈膝支撐，左腿屈膝提起，呈水平向前彈踢；左手直臂向後勾摟；目視前方。（圖 45）

(4) Keep the above action, swing the right palm by backhand forward through the front of the chest. At the same time, squats the body slightly; bend the right knee to support the body; bend the left knee and raise the left leg to horizontally kick forward. Grab the left hand backward with the left arm straight. Eyes look forward.（Figure 45）

圖 46

## 22. 縮身七星
### Shrink body in seven–star stance

接上勢。左腳落地，右腳內側裏扣，左腳尖裏側成七星步；右掌立掌於左肩上方，掌心向左，掌指與頷同平；左掌直臂向裏格掌於左膝前；目視前方。（圖 46）

要點：上步、下蹲和立掌要協調連貫。

七星小架套路動作圖解

　　Follow the above posture, the left foot falls to the ground. Turn the inner side of the right foot and the left tiptoe inward into seven –star stance. Stand the right palm above the left shoulder, keep the palm leftward and the fingers at jaw height; parry inward with the left palm to the front of the left knee with the left arm straight. Eyes look forward. ( Figure 46 )

　　Key points: stepping forward, squatting the body and standing palm shall be coherent and harmony.

七星小架

圖 47

## 23. 護耳掌 Ear-guarding palm

接上勢。左腳向左上步，同時，身體右轉 90°成馬步；右拳回抱於腰間；左掌屈肘格掌於左耳側，掌心向前；目視左方。（圖 47、圖 47 附圖）

要點：格掌要擰腰抖肩發力，與開左腳要同時進行。

圖 47 附圖

Follow the above posture, the left foot steps forward. At the same time, turn the body 90° to the right into horse stance; draw the right fist back and hold it on the waist; bend the left elbow to parry the left palm at the side of the left ear with the palm forward. Eyes look forward. (Figure 47, Attached figure 47)

Key points: when parrying the palm, twist the waist and snap the shoulders to send strength, which shall be simultaneously done with putting the left foot apart from the right one.

圖 48

## 24. 震腳盤肘　Stamp foot and bend elbow

接上勢。身體左轉 180°，震右腳併步，身體下蹲；右臂屈肘，隨身轉向左盤肘；左掌與右肘合抱於胸前；目視左掌。（圖 48）

要點：左掌和右肘合抱要抖肩發力，有合力。

Follow the above posture, turn the body 180° to the left. Stamp the right foot and put the feet together. The body squats, bend the right elbow to cross it with the left arm with body turn; hold the left palm and the right elbow together in front of the chest. Eyes look at the left palm. 〔Figure 48〕

Key points: when holding the left palm and the right elbow together, send shoulders to apply force, there shall be resultant force.

圖 49

## 25. 外擺腿  Swing leg outward

接上勢。右轉身，右腳向前、向外擺踢；同時，雙臂自然分開，左右手依次迎擊腳面；目視右腳。（圖 49）

要點：外擺腿要直、要高，輕靈而快捷。

Follow the above posture, turn the body to the right, and swing the right leg outward ahead. At the same time, the two hands part naturally; the left hand and the right one counter punch the instep sequentially. Eyes look at the right foot. (Figure 49)

Key points: swinging the leg outward shall be straight and high, light and quick.

七星小架

圖 50

## 26. 弓步沖拳　Thrust fist in bow stance

(1)接上勢。右腳在身體右側落步；左拳抱於腰間，拳心向上；右掌置於左胸前；目視右方。（圖50）

(1)Follow the above posture, the right foot falls at the right side of the body. Hold the left fist on the waist with the fist – palm up, place the right palm in front of the chest. Eyes look rightward.（Figure 50）

七星小架套路動作圖解

圖 51

（2）上動不停。右轉身 90°成弓步；同時，右掌向外
摟抓變拳回抱於腰間；左拳向前直臂沖出，拳心向
下，拳眼向右，高與肩平；目視前方。（圖 51）

要點：沖拳要抖肩發力，力達拳面。

（2）Keep the above action, turn the body 90° to the right into
bow stance. At the same time, grab the right palm outward into
fist, draw back the fist and hold it on the waist; punch the left fist
forward with the left arm straight, keep the fist–palm down and
the fist– hole rightward, at shoulder height. Eyes look forward.
（Figure 51）

Key points: when punching the fist, send the shoulders to
apply force that shall reach the fist–plane.

圖 52

## 27. 馬步截拳　Intercept with fist in horse stance

(1)接上勢。左轉身 90°成馬步；同時，左拳變掌，經面前向左格擋；目視左方。（圖 52）

(1) Follow the above posture, turn the body 90° to the left into stance. At the same time, change the right fist into palm and parry it leftward through the front of faces; hold the right fist on the waist. Eyes look leftward.（Figure 52）

七星小架套路動作圖解

圖 53

(2)上動不停。左掌變拳回抱腰間;同時,右擰身,身體右傾;右拳屈肘向右下截拳,拳心向下;目視右拳。(圖 53)

(2) Keep the above action, change the left palm into fist and hold it on the waist. At the same time, twist and slant the body rightward, bend the right elbow and swing the right fist right downward with the fist–palm down. Eyes look at the right fist. 〔Figure 53〕

圖 54

## 28. 裹裹手　Wrap the hand inward

(1)接上勢。身體左轉 90°，同時，提腿收右腳；左拳仍抱於腰間；右拳隨身轉；目視右拳。（圖 54）

(1)Follow the above posture, turn the body 90° to the left. At the same time, raise the right leg to draw back the right foot; still hold the left fist on the waist; turn the right one with body turn. Eyes look at the right fist. ( Figure 54 )

圖 55

　　(2)上動不停。右腳震腳，併步下蹲；右拳直臂內旋，裹手於雙膝前，拳心向右；目視前下方。（圖55）

　　要點：動作要連貫協調，快速有力。

　　(2) Keep the above action, stamp the right foot and put the feet together, squat the body. Rotate the right fist inward with the right arm straight, wrap the hand to the front of the two knees with the fist –palm rightward. Eyes look downward ahead. (Figure 55)

　　Key points: the action shall be coherent and consistent, quick and forceful.

圖 56

# 第四段　Section　Four

### 29. 馬步截拳　Intercept with fist in horse stance

接上勢。右腳向右開一步成馬步；同時，右拳屈肘向右下方截拳；左拳抱於腰間，拳心向下，拳眼向左；目視右下方。（圖 56）

Follow the above posture, the right foot steps a step rightward into horse stance. At the same time, bend the right elbow and swing the right fist right downward; hold the left fist on the waist, keep the fist –palm down and the fist –hole leftward. Eyes look right downward.（Figure 56）

圖 57

## 30. 馬步撞肘　Strike with elbow in horse stance

接上勢。右拳屈肘回收於胸前，向右撞肘，臂與肩平；目視右方。（圖 57）

要點：撞肘要抖肩發力，力達前臂外側。

Follow the above posture, bend the right elbow to draw back the right fist to the front of the chest, strike rightward with the elbow, the right arm shall be at shoulder height. Eyes look rightward.（Figure 57）

Key points: when striking with elbow, send the shoulders to apply force, which shall reach the outer side of the forearm.

圖 58

## 31. 弓步扳手
## Press hand in bow stance

接上勢。右轉身 90°成右弓步；同時，右拳變掌，屈臂向前反背扳掌，掌心向裏，掌指向上；目視右掌。（圖 58）

要點：扳掌要短促有力。

七星小架套路動作圖解

Follow the above posture, turn the body 90° to the right into right bow stance. At the same time, change the right fist into palm and bend the arm to swing and press the palm with backhand, keep the palm inward and the fingers upward. Move the barycenter forward; still hold the left palm on the waist. Eyes look at the right palm. ( Figure 58 )

Key points: turning round the palm shall be transient and forceful.

七星小架

圖 59

## 32. 十字彈腿　Cross snap kick

（1）接上勢。右掌上挑，高與頷平；左掌變拳，附於右肘內側；目視前方。（圖 59）

(1) Follow the above posture, the right palm and thrusts upward, at chin height; change the left palm into fist and keep it close to the inner side of the right elbow. Eyes look forward. （Figure 59）

圖 60

(2)上動不停。右掌向外、向下攪手於腹前；弓步不變；目視前方。（圖60）

(2) Keep the above action, agitate the right palm outward and downward to the front of the abdomen. Keep in bow stance. Eyes look forward.〔Figure 60〕

圖 61

（3）上動不停。左掌直臂下按；右掌回收於左腋下；微起身；目視前下方。（圖 61）

(3) Keep the above action, press the left palm downward with the arm straight; draw back the right palm under the left armpit. Slightly raise the body. Eyes look downward ahead. 〔Figure 61〕

七星小架套路動作圖解

圖 62

（4）上動不停。右掌旋即從左腋下抽出，向前反背擊出；左手向後、向上勾摟，手心向上；同時，身體下蹲，左腿屈膝提起向前彈踢，右腿屈膝支撐；目視前方。（圖 62）

(4) Keep the above action, draw out the right palm from under the left armpit immediately, punch it forward with backhand; grab the left hand backward and upward with the palm up. At the same time, squat the body, bend the left knee to raise the left foot and kick it forward; bend the right knee to support the body. Eyes look forward.〔Figure 62〕

圖 63

### 33. 縮身七星
Shrink body in seven–star stance

　　接上勢。左腳落地，身體下蹲，右腳內側裏扣左腳尖裏側成七星步；同時，右掌經胸前屈肘立掌於左肩上方，高與頜平；左掌直臂向裏格掌於左膝前；目視前方。（圖63）

七星小架套路動作圖解

Follow the above posture, the left foot lands to the ground, squat the body. Turn the inner side of the right foot and the left tiptoe inward into seven-star stance. At the same time, bend the right elbow and stand the right palm above the left shoulder, at chin height; parry inward with the left palm, the arm straight. Eyes look forward. 〔 Figure 63 〕

圖 64

## 34. 二起腳　Jumping kick twice

(1)接上勢。雙腳蹬地跳起，右腳向前、向上彈踢；右手向前拍擊腳面；左拳回抱於腰間；目視右腳。（圖 64）

(1)Follow the above posture, the two feet press against the ground to jump up, the right foot kicks upward ahead. The right hand claps the instep forward; draw back the left fist and hold it on the waist. Eyes look at the right foot.（Figure 64）

圖 65

（2）上動不停。右腳落地；雙手自然下落，手心向後；目視前方。（圖 65）

(2) Keep the above action, the right foot lands to the ground; the two hands drop naturally with the palm backward. Shift the barycenter backward. Eyes look forward.〔Figure 65〕

七星小架

圖 66

　　(3)上動不停。左轉身 180°，同時，左腳跳步提膝，右腿直立；雙拳屈肘抱於胸前，拳心向裏，拳眼向外，高與肩平；目視左方。（圖 66、圖 66 附圖）

　　要點：二起腳騰空要高，拍擊力點要準確響亮。

七星小架套路動作圖解

圖 66 附圖

(3) Keep the above action, turn the body 180° to the left. At the same time, the left foot jumps to lift the knee; the right leg stands upright. Bend the two elbows and hold the two fists in front of the chest, keep the fist–palm inward and the fist–hole outward, at shoulder level. Eyes look leftward. ( Figure 66, Attached figure 66 )

Key points: jumping kick twice shall be high, the strength of the slap shall be accurate and clangorous.

七星小架

圖 67

## 35. 十字沖拳　Thrust cross fists

(1)接上勢。左腳向左落步成仆步；雙拳姿勢不變；目視左下方。（圖 67、圖 67 附圖）

七星小架套路動作圖解

圖 67 附圖

(1)Follow the above posture, the left foot lands left–ward into crouch stance. Keep the posture of the two fists. Eyes look left downward.（Figure 67, Attached figure 67）

圖 68

(2)上動不停。左轉身成左弓步；雙拳經腰間向左右兩側沖擊，拳心向下，高與肩平；目視左方。（圖68）

(2) Keep the above action, turn the body to the left into left bow stance. Punch the two fists to the both sides of the body from the waist with the fist–palm down, at shoulder height. Eyes look leftward．〔Figure 68〕

圖 69

## 36. 縮身七星　Shrink body in seven-star stance

接上勢。右轉身 180°，收左腳成七星步；雙拳變
掌，右掌經胸前屈肘立掌於左肩上方；左掌直臂向右
格掌於左膝前；目平視左方。（圖 69）

要點：動作要連貫協調，輕靈迅猛。


Follow the above posture, turn the body 180° to the right,
draw back the left foot into seven–star stance. Change the two
fists into palms. Bend the right palm through the front of the
chest and stand the palm above the left shoulder, parry the left
palm rightward with the arm straight to the front of the left knee.
Eyes look horizontally leftward.（Figure 69）

　　Key points: the action shall be coherent and harmony, light
and swift.

圖 70

## 37. 上步兩沖拳　Step forward and punch twice

（1）接上勢。左腳向前上步，成馬步；同時，左手抱拳於胸前；右掌下按於左拳前，掌心向下；目視雙手。（圖 70）

（1）Follow the above posture, the left foot steps for–ward into horse stance. At the same time, hold the left fist to the front of the chest, press the right palm before the left fist with the palm down. Eyes look at the two hands.（Figure 70）

圖71

(2)上動不停。右拳回抱腰間；左拳前沖，拳心向下，拳眼向右，與肩同高；目視前方。（圖71）

(2)Keep the above action, draw back the right fist and hold it on the waist; punch the left fist forward, keep the fist‑palm down and the fist‑hole rightward, at shoulder height. Eyes look forward.〔Figure 71〕

七星小架

圖 72

(3)上動不停。右腳向前一步，同時，左轉身成馬步；左拳變掌，下按於右拳前，掌心向下；目視右前下方。（圖72）

(3) Keep the above action, the right foot takes a step forward. At the same time, change the left fist into palm and press it to the front of the right fist with the palm down. Eyes look right downward ahead.〔Figure 72〕

七星小架套路動作圖解

圖 73

(4)上動不停。左掌抱拳於腰間；同時，右拳向前沖出，拳心向下，與肩同高；目視前方。（圖73）

要點：沖拳要擰腰抖肩發力，力達拳面。

(4) Keep the above action, change the left palm into fist and hold it on the waist. At the same time, thrust the right fist forward, keep the fist–palm down, at shoulder height. Eyes look forward.（Figure 73）

Key points: when punching the fist, twist the waist and send the shoulder to apply force that shall reach the fist–plane.

七星小架

圖 74

## 38. 馬步剪子手
## Scissors hand in horse stance

（1）接上勢。右拳回抱腰間；同時，左轉身 180°，左手直臂經胸前向外摟抓；身體前傾；目視左手。（圖 74）

七星小架套路動作圖解

(1) Follow the above posture, draw back the right fist and hold it on the waist. At the same time, turn the body 180° to the left, grab the left hand outward through the front of the chest with the arm straight. Lean the body forward. Eyes look at the left hand. ( Figure 74 )

七星小架

圖 75

(2)上動不停。左手回收腰間成拳；同時，左轉身180°，右腳向前上一步成馬步；右拳食指、中指伸直分開，其餘手指扣攏成剪子手向前插擊，臂與肩平；目視右方。（圖 75）

要點：馬步要穩固，剪子手要抖肩發力，力達雙指。

七星小架套路動作圖解

(2) Keep the above action, draw back the left hand and hold it on the waist into fist. At the same time, turn the body 180° to the left, the right foot takes a step forward into horse stance · Stretch and detach the forefinger, middle finger of the right fist, hold other fingers together into scissors hand and pierce forward, the arm and the shoulder shall be at the same level. Eyes look rightward. ( Figure 75 )

Key points: the horse stance shall be stable, send the shoulders to apply force for the scissors hand, the force shall reach the two fingers.

七星小架

圖76

## 39. 馬步七星
## Seven-star in horse stance

接上勢。右剪子手回收，經小腹前向上在胸前屈肘立掌，掌心向左，指尖與咽喉同高；同時，左掌經右臂內側直臂下插於襠前護襠，掌心向內；馬步不變，口發「嗯」聲；目視前方。（圖76）

七星小架套路動作圖解

Follow the above posture, draw back the right scissors hand through the front of the lower abdomen, bend the elbow in front of the chest and stand the palm upward with the palm leftward, and the fingertip shall be at throat height. At the same time, insert the left palm downward through the inner side of the right arm to the front of the crotch in order to guard the crotch with the palm inward. Keep in horse stance. The mouth makes the sound of "en". Eyes look forward. ( Figure 76 )

圖 77

## 40. 收勢 Closing form

（1）接上勢。雙掌經胸前交叉，然後向上、向外環繞分掌；馬步不變；目視右方。（圖 77）

（1）Follow the above posture, cross the two palms through the front of the chest, and then encircle the two palms upward and outward to detach them. Keep in the horse stance. Eyes look rightward.（Figure 77）

七星小架套路動作圖解

圖 78

(2)上動不停。雙掌屈肘回抱腰間變拳，拳心向
上；左腳回收成併步；目視前方。（圖 78）

(2)Keep the above action, bend the elbows to draw back the
two palms and hold it on the waist with the fist－palms up. Draw
back the left foot and put the feet together. Eyeslook forward.
〔Figure 78〕

七星小架

圖 79

(3)上動不停。兩手五指併攏，自然下垂在身體兩側，成立正姿勢；目視前方。（圖 79）

要點：心平氣和，體態自然。

(3) Keep the above action, put the five fingers of each hand together, hunging naturally at both sides of the body, and stand at attention. Eyes look forward. (Figure 79)

Key points: be calm and comfortable in natural posture.

全套動作示意圖

# Demonstration of All the Action

圖 1　圖 2　圖 3　圖 4　圖 5

圖 6　圖 7　圖 8　圖 9　圖 10　圖 10 附圖

全套動作示意圖

圖 15

圖 14

圖 13

圖 12

圖 11

圖 19

圖 18

圖 17

圖 16

七星小架

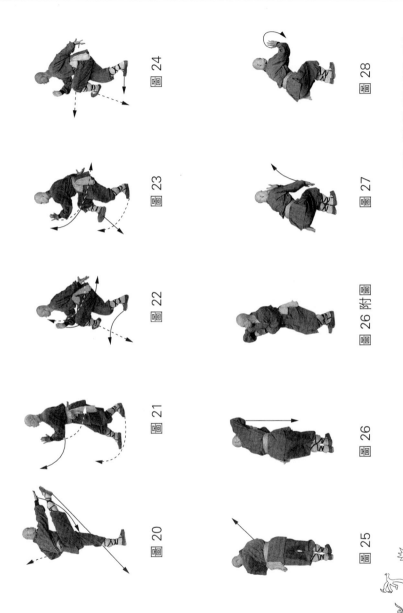

全套動作示意圖

七星小架

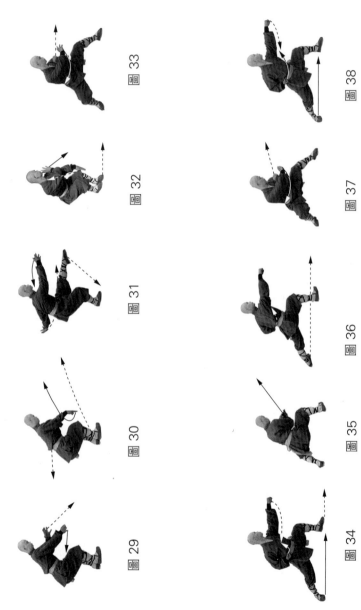

圖 33

圖 32

圖 31

圖 30

圖 29

圖 38

圖 37

圖 36

圖 35

圖 34

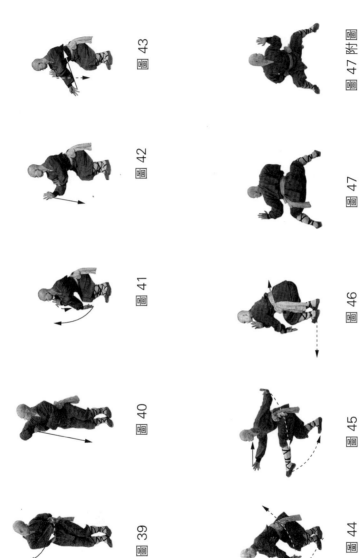

全套動作示意圖

圖 43

圖 42

圖 41

圖 40

圖 39

圖 47 附

圖 47

圖 46

圖 45

圖 44

七星小架

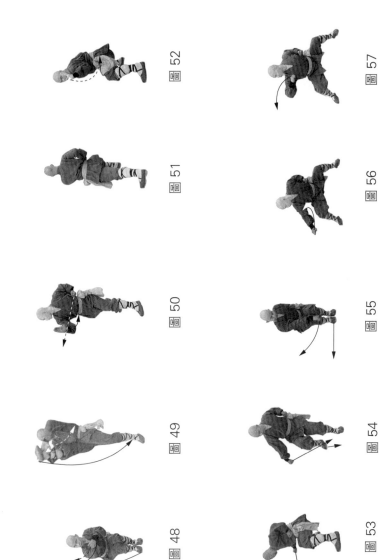

圖 52

圖 57

圖 51

圖 56

圖 50

圖 55

圖 49

圖 54

圖 48

圖 53

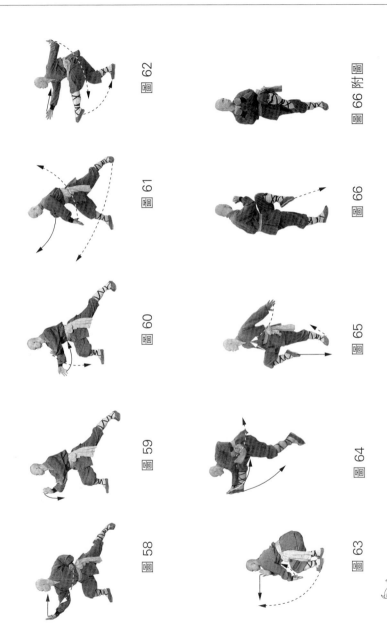

圖 62

附 圖 66

圖 61

圖 66

圖 60

圖 65

圖 59

圖 64

圖 58

圖 63

全套動作示意圖

七星小架

圖 70

圖 69

圖 68

圖 67 附圖

圖 67

圖 75

圖 74

圖 73

圖 72

圖 71

全套動作示意圖

图 79

图 78

图 77

图 76

# 導引養生功 系列叢書

張廣德養生著作

每冊定價 350 元

全系列為彩色圖解附教學光碟

# 彩色圖解太極武術

1 太極功夫扇
定價220元

2 武當太極劍
定價220元

3 楊式太極劍
定價220元

4 楊式太極刀
定價220元

5 二十四式太極拳+VCD
定價350元

6 三十二式太極劍+VCD
定價350元

7 四十二式太極劍+VCD
定價350元

8 四十二式太極拳+VCD
定價350元

9 楊式十八式太極劍
定價350元

10 楊氏二十八式太極拳+VCD
定價350元

11 楊式太極拳四十式+VCD
定價350元

12 陳式太極拳五十六式+VCD
定價350元

13 吳式太極拳五十六式+VCD
定價350元

14 精簡陳式太極拳八式十六式
定價220元

15 精簡吳式太極拳架·推手三十六式
定價220元

16 夕陽美功夫扇
定價220元

17 綜合四十八式太極拳+VCD
定價350元

18 三十二式太極拳 四段
定價220元

19 楊式三十七式太極拳+VCD
定價350元

20 楊氏五十一式太極劍+VCD
定價350元

## 太極跤

1 太極防身術

定價300元

2 擒拿術

定價280元

3 中國式摔角

定價350元

## 簡化太極拳

1 陳式太極拳十三式

定價200元

2 楊式太極拳十三式

定價200元

3 吳式太極拳十三式

定價200元

4 武式太極拳十三式

定價200元

5 孫式太極拳十三式

定價200元

6 趙堡太極拳十三式

定價200元

## 原地太極拳

1 原地綜合太極拳二十四式

定價220元

2 原地活步太極拳四十二式

定價200元

3 原地簡化太極拳二十四式

定價200元

4 原地太極拳十二式

定價200元

5 原地青少年太極拳二十二式

定價220元

6 原地兒童太極拳十捶十六式

定價180元

# 健康加油站

1 糖尿病預防與治療

定價200元

2 胃部機能與強健

定價180元

3 不孕症治療

定價200元

4 簡易醫學急救法

定價200元

5 肥胖健康診療

定價200元

6 肝功能健康診療

定價200元

7 高血壓健康診療

定價200元

8 高血糖值健康診療

定價200元

9 尿酸值健康診療

定價200元

10 膽固醇中性脂肪健康診療

定價200元

11 痛風劇痛消除法

定價180元

12 三溫暖健康法

定價180元

13 手・腳病理按摩

定價180元

14 B型肝炎預防與治療

定價180元

15 吃得更漂亮、健康

定價180元

16 茶使您更健康

定價180元

17 圖解常見疾病運動療法

定價180元

18 科學健身改變亞健康

定價180元

19 簡易萬病自療保健

定價220元

20 王朝秘藥媚酒

定價180元

# 運動精進叢書

1 怎樣跑得快

定價200元

2 怎樣投得遠
定價180元

3 怎樣跳得遠
定價180元

4 怎樣跳的高

定價180元

5 高爾夫揮桿原理

定價220元

6 網球技巧圖解
定價220元

7 排球技巧圖解

定價230元

8 沙灘排球技巧圖解

定價230元

9 撞球技巧圖解

定價230元

10 籃球技巧圖解

定價220元

11 足球技巧圖解

定價230元

12 羽毛球技巧圖解

定價220元

13 乒乓球技巧圖解

定價220元

14 曲線球與飛碟球

定價300元

15 街頭花式籃球

定價280元

16 精彩高爾夫

定價330元

17 巴西青少年足球訓練方法

定價230元

# 快樂健美站

1 柔力健身球

定價280元

2 自行車健康享瘦

定價280元

3 跑步鍛鍊走路減肥

定價280元

4 創造健康的肌力訓練

定價220元

5 舒適超級伸展體操

定價280元

6 水中有氧運動

定價280元

7 雕塑完美身材

定價280元

8 創造超級兒童

定價280元

9 使頭腦變聰明

定價280元

10 防止老化的身體改造訓練

定價280元

11 三個月塑身計畫

定價280元

12 懶人族瑜伽

定價280元

13 忙裡偷閒練瑜伽基礎篇

定價240元

14 忙裡偷閒練瑜伽袪病養生篇

定價240元

15 健身跑激發身體的潛能

定價200元

16 中華鐵球健身操

定價180元

17 彼拉提斯健身寶典

定價280元

18 全身保健操＋VCD

定價280元

19 瑜伽美姿美容

定價180元

20 豐胸做自信女人

定價200元

21 輕鬆瑜伽治百病

定價280元

# 常見病藥膳調養叢書

1 脂肪肝四季飲食
定價200元

2 高血壓四季飲食
定價200元

3 慢性腎炎四季飲食
定價200元

4 高脂血症四季飲食
定價200元

5 慢性胃炎四季飲食
定價200元

6 糖尿病四季飲食
定價200元

7 癌症四季飲食
定價200元

8 痛風四季飲食
定價200元

9 肝炎四季飲食
定價200元

10 肥胖症四季飲食
定價200元

11 膽囊炎、膽石症四季飲食
定價200元

# 傳統民俗療法

1 神奇刀療法
定價200元

2 神奇拍打療法
定價200元

3 神奇拔罐療法
定價200元

4 神奇艾灸療法
定價200元

5 神奇貼敷療法
定價200元

6 神奇薰洗療法
定價200元

7 神奇耳穴療法
定價200元

8 神奇指針療法
定價200元

9 神奇藥酒療法
定價200元

10 神奇藥茶療法
定價200元

11 神奇推拿療法
定價200元

12 神奇止痛療法
定價200元

13 神奇天然藥食物療法
定價200元

14 神奇新穴療法
定價200元

15 神奇小針刀療法
定價200元

16 神奇刮痧療法
定價200元

品冠文化出版社

國家圖書館出版品預行編目資料

七星小架／耿　軍　著
——初版，——臺北市，大展，2007〔民96〕
面；21公分，——（少林傳統功夫漢英對照系列；6）
ISBN　978-957-468-553-0（平裝）
1.拳術—中國
528.97　　　　　　　　　　　　　　　96010850

# 七星小架

ISBN　978-957-468-553-0

著　　者／耿　軍
責任編輯／張　建　林
發 行 人／蔡　森　明
出 版 者／大展出版社有限公司
社　　址／台北市北投區（石牌）致遠一路2段12巷1號
電　　話／（02）28236031・28236033・28233123
傳　　眞／（02）28272069
郵政劃撥／01669551
網　　址／www.dah-jaan.com.tw
E – mail ／ service@dah-jaan.com.tw
登 記 證／局版臺業字第2171號
承 印 者／高星印刷品行
裝　　訂／建鑫印刷裝訂有限公司
排 版 者／弘益電腦排版有限公司
授 權 者／北京人民體育出版社
初版1刷／2007年（民96年）8月

定　價／180元

大展好書　好書大展
品嘗好書　冠群可期

大展好書　好書大展

品嘗好書　冠群可期